D1275713

Step by Step

Snacks

Snacks

Janet Marsh Lillie

Bloomsbury Books
London

Page two: Pissaladière (p.36)—a hearty pizza with onions, olives and anchovies.The endpapers show the pissaladière with the onion mixture spread over the dough, and the anchovies and olives about to be placed.

This edition published in 1994 by
Bloomsbury Books
an imprint of
The Godfrey Cave Group
42 Bloomsbury Street, London. WC1B 3QJ
under license from
Harlaxton Publishing Limited

Harlaxton Publishing Limited
2 Avenue Road, Grantham, Lincolnshire, NG31 6TA
United Kingdom
A Member of the Weldon International Group of Companies

First Published in 1994

Publisher: Robin Burgess
Project Coordinator: Barbara Beckett
Designer: Rachel Rush
Edited by: Jo Jarrah and Alison Leach
Illustrator: Maggie Renvoize
Jacket photographer: Rodney Weidland
Inside photography: Jack Sarafian
Food stylist: Janet Marsh Lillie
Produced by Barbara Beckett Publishing
Colour Separation: G.A. Graphics, Stamford, UK
Printer: Imago, Singapore

British Library Cataloguing-in-Publication data.
A catalogue record for this book is available from the British Library

Title: Step by Step, SNACKS
ISBN: 1 85471 333 7

Step by Step

Contents

Cook's Notes 6
Measurements and Ingredients

Introduction 9

Cold Sandwich Snacks 10

Hot Sandwich Snacks 16

Dips and Spreads 21

Egg Snacks 31

Pizzas 36

Light Meal Snacks 42

Glossary 47

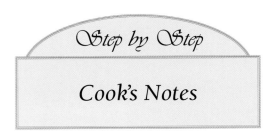

Cook's Notes

Measurements

All spoon and cup measurements are level. Standard spoon and cup measures are used in all the recipes. I recommend using a graduated nest of measuring cups: 1 cup, ½ cup, ⅓ cup and ¼ cup. The graduated nest of spoons comprises 1 tablespoon, 1 teaspoon, ½ teaspoon and ¼ teaspoon. For liquids, use a standard litre or imperial pint measuring jug that also shows cup measurements. As the metric/imperial/US/equivalents given are not exact, follow only one system of measurement within the recipe.

Ovens should be preheated to the specified temperature. When cooking on the hob (stove plate), use medium heat where high, low or simmer are not specified.

Ingredients

Fresh **fruit** and **vegetables** should be used in the recipes unless otherwise stated. **Herb** quantities are for fresh herbs; if fresh are unobtainable, use half the quantity of dried herbs. Use freshly ground black **pepper** whenever pepper is listed; use **salt** and pepper to individual taste; use plain (all-purpose) **flour** unless otherwise stated. Use fresh **chillies**; if substituting dried chillies halve the quantity or add to individual taste. Cold-pressed virgin olive **oil** is recommended, but any type may be used. Use unsalted **butter** if available, or **margarine** if more practical for spreading on breads etc. Well-known brands of **canned** foods such as **tuna**, **tomatoes** and **beans** of different kinds have been used.

Spaghetti Carbonara (p. 46). Any pasta may be used to make this popular dish, so it can become a favourite standby snack meal.

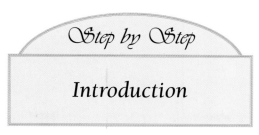

Introduction

What is a snack? It seems everyone has their own interpretation. It can be as simple as an apple, a homemade scone, a slice of toast oozing with honey, grilled (broiled) cheese on a muffin, hot take-away (take-out) burger and chips... Something as basic hardly needs any planning much less a recipe, you may say. However, this book will introduce you to serious sandwiches with wonderful, easy-to-prepare fillings; piping hot pizzas of different shapes and styles; easy egg recipes; dips and crudités; and snacks suitable for light meals. Some are based on the classic combinations —favourites that have stood the test of time—and others bring together selections of ready-prepared ingredients, so the task of making snacks is easy and fun, and eating them an enjoyable experience.

This book will teach you how to prepare snacks even if you have never cooked before. It explains the basic steps as well as cooking techniques you may not have tried before or feel a little nervous about trying.

The instructions are clearly set out. There are step-by-step guides to the different cooking methods, such as omelette and pasta cooking. Many recipes are photographed in preparation to show a special technique as well as what the finished dish looks like and how to present it for the table. Detailed step-by-step drawings also illustrate making an omelette, cooking pasta or making a pizza base. There are handy hints set off in boxes, giving information such as how to crush garlic, blanch vegetables and stone (pit) olives.

A glossary of cooking terms begins on page 47 for you to look up any term that is unfamiliar. There is a list of recipes on page 5 for your reference. Be sure to read the information on measurements and ingredients on page 6.

One of the most important things to do when trying a new recipe is to read the recipe very thoroughly before starting. Check that you have all the ingredients, and make an estimate of the amount of time needed. Have you time to prepare a caesar salad? Or would it be better simply to prepare one of the delicious sandwich recipes?

No unusual or particular equipment is required to prepare snacks but ensure you have basics in your kitchen such as a chopping board, a vegetable peeler, a grater, bowls of varying sizes, sieve (strainer), whisk, wooden spoons, a good set of sharp knives including a serrated knife for cutting bread, a wire cake rack, bun tins (muffin pans), baking sheets, a rolling pin, at least two heavy-based saucepans of different sizes, a frying pan (skillet), a small non-stick omelette pan, a pastry brush, screw-topped jars, cocktail sticks (toothpicks), foil, string, paper towels polythene, bags and a food processor or blender, though not essential, can save so much time and energy.

A squeeze of lemon juice and some freshly ground pepper add the final touch to Sun-Dried Grilled Vegetable Pizza (p. 41).

Cold Sandwich Snacks

There are sandwiches as simple as a slice of cheese or meat with pickle or mustard slapped between two sheets of white bread. On the other hand, you can raid the refrigerator or larder (pantry) and make a triple-decker ribbon or a 'dagwood'. While sandwiches are as easy to prepare as they are to eat, it is possible, with a little more care and planning, to make them innovative, really appetizing and a pleasure to serve to family and friends.

The most essential ingredient is good quality bread. No longer is there just white bread. Markets and bakeries abound with bread of every conceivable size, shape and style. Breads full of fibre, wholegrains, herbs, cracked wheat, dark and light rye, or unbleached flours have created new textures and flavours which you can choose as a sandwich base.

You do not have to use butter or margarine as a spread—instead, enjoy experimenting with olive oil, cream or ricotta cheeses, mayonnaise or mashed, seasoned avocado as a starting point to protect the bread from moist toppings and to add flavour to crisp salads, meats, eggs and tuna.

Italian Lunch Loaf (p. 14) in preparation. Look for a round or oblong well-shaped loaf with a hard crust—it is easier to prepare and fill.

Avocado Spread

Place the flesh of half a ripe avocado and 125 g/4 oz cream cheese in a food processor, and blend until smooth. Add ¼ teaspoon ground cumin, 6 teaspoons lemon juice and season with salt. Process again until combined.
Makes about 1 cup

Salad Stack on Rye

A mustard-walnut cheese replaces other spreads in this novel sandwich. You can vary the ingredients to suit what you have available-choose Cheddar, feta or Gruyère cheeses instead of meat, or sliced pimento and dill cucumber to add variety.

250 g/9 oz/generous 1 cup cream cheese, softened
2–3 tablespoons seed mustard
60 g/2 oz/½ cup walnuts, finely chopped
Salt and pepper
16 slice dark or light rye bread
8–12 lettuce leaves

1 large carrot, cut into strips
8 slices ham or mortadella, or 16 slices salami
8 slices tomato
8 diagonally-cut slices cucumber
Italian (flat leaf) parsley sprigs

Beat together the cream cheese and mustard until smooth and creamy. Stir in the walnuts. Season with salt and pepper. Spread the mixture over one side of each bread slice. Assemble 8 sandwiches, starting with the lettuce, then carrot, meat, tomato, cucumber and 2–3 parsley sprigs. Close the sandwiches by pressing firmly together, and arrange them on a board or platter. If you have used an unsliced loaf, stack the sandwiches in order of size to resemble the original loaf.
Makes 8

Making Sandwiches

| Cut loaf into 16 slices. | Place on board and spread on cream cheese mixture. | Lay down the filling and place slice of bread over the top. | Press sandwich firmly and slice as liked. |

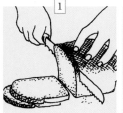

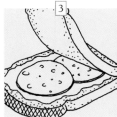

Crushing Garlic. *Place the unpeeled garlic clove on a board. Place the flat part of the knife blade on top and give the blade a sharp hit with the side of your hand. This will flatten the clove and make the skin easy to peel. Sprinkle the garlic with 1 teaspoon of salt and chop finely or crush using a garlic press.*

Niçoise Salad Rolls

Enjoy this Provençal-style colourful tuna salad with the cooked potatoes as a filling for crusty French bread or wholemeal rolls.

250 g/9 oz whole French (green beans), trimmed, cut in half
3 tomatoes, cut into wedges
200 g/7 oz canned tuna chunks in brine, drained
8 black olives, stoned (pitted)
125 g/4 oz baby spinach or small leaves of cos (romaine) lettuce
4 tablespoons olive oil

2 tablespoons cider or tarragon vinegar
1 garlic clove, crushed
Salt and pepper
4 crusty sticks of bread or rolls, 15–20 cm/6–8 inches long
2 hard-boiled eggs (p. 13), cut in halves or quarters, to garnish

Cook the beans in a saucepan of boiling water for 4–5 minutes, drain in a sieve (strainer) and rinse in cold water. Place in a bowl and add the tomatoes, tuna, olives and spinach or lettuce. Place the olive oil, vinegar and garlic in a small bowl or screw-topped jar. Stir vigorously or shake together, then season with salt and pepper. Toss through the salad. Cut the sticks of bread or rolls almost in half horizontally, open out and fill with the salad mixture. Garnish with egg and spoon over any leftover dressing.
Serves 4

Assembling Salad Rolls

| *Place salad ingredients in a bowl.* | *Mix dressing and toss through salad.* | *Cut roll in half horizontally.* | *Place filling on bottom half of roll and replace the top.* |

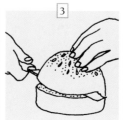

Caper Egg Bruschetta with Tomatoes—an unusual open sandwich using stuffed eggs.

Caper Egg Bruschetta with Tomatoes

Bruschetta is toasted bread rubbed with a garlic clove, then drenched in olive oil and sprinkled with crystalline (rock) salt. You will definitely need a knife and fork to enjoy this open-style sandwich.

4 eggs
3 tablespoons chopped parsley
1 clove garlic, crushed
3 teaspoons capers, drained
5–6 tablespoons olive oil
4 thick diagonally-cut slices coarse country-style
    bread

3 large ripe tomatoes, sliced
Salt and pepper
Basil leaves, to garnish
Thin onion rings, to garnish
4 anchovy fillets if liked, to garnish

To hard-boil eggs. Place the eggs in a large saucepan and cover with water. Bring to the boil and cook for about 12–15 minutes. Pour off the water and hold the eggs under a stream of cold running water until cool. When cold, tap gently on a hard surface to break the shell, peel, and cut each egg in half.

Remove the egg yolks carefully and leave the egg white shells aside. Place the yolks in a bowl and mash, adding the parsley, garlic, capers and 4–6 teaspoons of the olive oil. Spoon back into the egg white shells. Toast the bread lightly under a grill (broiler). Brush with the remaining oil, top with tomato slices, season with salt and pepper. Top each slice with 2 stuffed egg halves, basil leaves, a few onion rings and an anchovy fillet.

Serves 4

Italian Lunch Loaf

This hearty sandwich is similar to the famous Muffuletta from New Orleans, combining tangy tapénade, sliced Italian-style meats, cheese and other seasonings layered as a filling in a loaf. You can select cheeses only if you wish.

1 hard-crusted white Italian loaf, measuring about
   30 x 15 cm/12 x 6 inches or 20 cm/8 inches round
Olive oil
5–6 tablespoons tapénade
250 g/9 oz mortadella, sliced
250 g/9 oz salami, sliced
6 fresh bocconcini, sliced (p. 47)

6 marinated or canned, drained artichoke hearts,
   sliced
20 basil leaves
250 g/9 oz whole button mushrooms, trimmed
8–10 sun-dried tomatoes
Salt and pepper

Cut the loaf in half horizontally near the top crust and remove some of the soft bread from each half to make room for the filling allowing 2.5 cm/1 inch shell. Press down the bread on the base to flatten it. Brush the inside of each half liberally with oil and spread with tapénade. Layer the meats, cheese and artichoke hearts in the bottom half of the loaf alternately with the basil, mushrooms and tomatoes. Season with salt and pepper.

Cover the filling with the top half of the loaf. Press down firmly over the filling. Tie the loaf together at intervals with string. Wrap the loaf in a tea-towel (dish cloth) or clingfilm (plastic wrap) and foil, and chill overnight with a weight on the top so the juices from the filling ingredients make the loaf moist.

Unwrap the loaf, snip the string, slice into eight triangles or wedges and serve in small napkins on a platter or in a basket.

Serves 4

Tapénade. Place 225 g/8 oz stoned (pitted) black olives, 2 peeled garlic cloves, 225 g/8 oz drained capers, 125 g/4 oz anchovy fillets (soaked for 10 minutes in milk if too salty), 1 teaspoon mustard and 3 teaspoons olive oil in a food processor and blend to a smooth paste. Place in an airtight jar or container and store in the refrigerator.

Makes about 2 1/4 cups

Stoning (Pitting) Olives. *With a small, sharp knife make a cut across the top of the olive, but not right through. Keeping the blade on the stone, cut round the whole olive lengthwise, then twist the two sides against each other to separate them. Using the tip of the knife, release the stone gently .*

Italian Lunch Loaf. Ensure your breadknife is sharp, so the filling stays in position when you cut the loaf. A complete snack lunch meal—ideal to take on a picnic and enjoy with a glass of red wine.

There is nothing more scrumptious than a hot, tasty satisfying snack. The days of using left-overs on or between toasted bread are past. You will find bakeries and supermarkets are specialist suppliers of any variety of textured and flavourful breads. Look for sour dough or rye loaves, crusty French bread, herb, olive and walnut rolls or make your own individually baked muffins.

Several of the following recipes use cheese—remember to preheat the grill (broiler) or oven because quick, instant heat will melt the cheese most successfully.

Croque Monsieur

A traditional French-style toasted cheese sandwich, a dash of mustard adds to its flavour.

125 g/4 oz/½ cup butter, softened
8 thick slices wholemeal (wholewheat), rye or
   white bread
2–3 tablespoons coarse-grain French mustard

4 thick slices lean ham
125 g/4 oz Cheddar or Gruyère cheese, thinly sliced
   or grated
Cress, to garnish

Spread the butter on the bread and cover with a thin layer of mustard. Place the ham and cheese onto 4 slices. Press the remaining slices on top to make a sandwich. Spread more butter generously on the outsides of each. Heat a large frying pan (skillet) and fry the sandwiches

Poaching Eggs

| Break an egg into a cup or onto a plate. | Gently slide it into a pan of simmering water. | Simmer for 2–3 minutes, until egg white is set. | Lift the egg out with an egg lifter or slotted spatula. |

  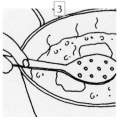 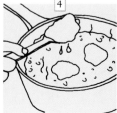

gently, turning after 1–2 minutes, until the cheese melts and the bread is golden on both sides. Garnish with cress and serve immediately.

Serves 4

Croque Madame. Use only 4 slices of bread and toast on one side only. Spread over the butter and mustard, and top with ham and cheese. Place under a grill (broiler) and cook until the cheese melts and bubbles. Top each with 1 poached egg and sprinkle with extra pepper.

To poach an egg, bring about 5 cm/2 inches of water to the boil in a frying pan (skillet) or saucepan. Break an egg on to a plate or into a cup. Slide the egg gently into the pan. Allow the water to simmer gently for 2–3 minutes, until the egg white is set. The white should be opaque and the yolk slightly set and covered by a layer of white. Lift out carefully from the pan with an egg slice and drain off the water.

Chopping Onions. *Using a small sharp knife, peel off the outer skin of the onion under a running tap or in a large bowl of cold water, leaving the root intact. Cut the onion in half vertically and lay the flat side on a board. Slice onion horizontally, not cutting the root, then turn the knife to its normal position and cut through vertically. Because you have cut the onion in two different directions, the result is perfect dice.*

Reuben on Rye

This hot sandwich, named after the traditions of Jewish cookery, is a favourite in many New York snack bars. You can purchase the sauerkraut in good delicatessens or supermarkets.

4 slices dark or light rye bread
4 tablespoons Thousand Island dressing
4 slices corned beef or smoked turkey

250 g/9 oz prepared sauerkraut
125 g/4 oz slices Gruyère or any Swiss cheese,
    cut into 4 slices

Place the rye bread under a preheated grill (broiler) and toast on one side only. Spread over the dressing and top each with a corned beef or turkey slice. Rinse the sauerkraut in cold water and squeeze dry. Divide between the slices and top with cheese. Grill until the topping heats through and the cheese melts completely.

Serves 4

Thousand Island Dressing. Combine together 125 ml/4 fl oz/½ cup egg-based mayonnaise, a dash of Tabasco, 1 small, finely chopped onion and 6 chopped stuffed olives. Season with salt and pepper.

Makes ½ cup

Butter-Capped Muffins—ham and corn add flavour and texture to these one bowl mix and bake quickbreads.

Bacon and Egg Baskets

You can use any number of toppings to add variety to this snack—grated Parmesan cheese, chopped tomato, stuffed olives, or a spoonful of cream are a few suggestions.

6 hamburger buns or round bread rolls
60 g/2 oz/¼ cup butter
2 teaspoons Worcestershire sauce
6 eggs

3 rashers (slices) bacon, rinds removed, finely
    chopped
1 onion, finely chopped
Salt and pepper

Cut a slice from the top of each bun or roll and set aside. Remove the soft bread from the centre carefully, leaving a 6 mm/1/4 inch shell. Melt the butter in a small saucepan and add the

Bacon and Egg Baskets

| Cut a slice from the top of each roll and remove the soft bread. | Brush the inside of each one with melted butter mixture. | Break in an egg. | Spoon in bacon and onion. Replace bread lids and brush rolls all over with butter. |

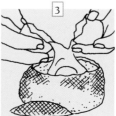

Worcestershire sauce. Brush the insides of each roll with some of the butter mixture. Break in an egg and place the rolls on a flat baking sheet. Cook the bacon and onion in a frying pan (skillet) for 3–4 minutes. Spoon over each egg. Season with salt and pepper. Replace the bread lids and brush any remaining butter mixture over the buns. Place in a preheated oven at 200°C/400°F/gas 6 and bake for 15–20 minutes until the buns are crisp. Serve hot or cold with a salad, or by themselves.

Makes 6

Butter-Capped Muffins

One bowl savoury or sweet quickbreads keep perfectly, sealed in polythene bags in your freezer, for any emergency snack.

225 g/8 oz/2 cups plain (all-purpose) flour	*250 ml/8 fl oz/1 cup milk*
3 teaspoons baking powder	*1 egg, lightly beaten*
½ teaspoon salt	*30 g/1 oz/2 tablespoons butter, melted*

Sift the flour, baking powder and salt into a large bowl. Mix together the milk, egg and butter, and pour them over the dry ingredients. Mix quickly, using a metal spoon, until the flour is just moistened—the mixture should still be lumpy. Spoon into well-greased medium-sized bun tins (muffin pans) filling them three-quarters full. Place in a preheated oven at 200 °C/400°F/gas 6 and bake for 20–25 minutes or until the muffins are well risen and golden. Loosen the edges if necessary and turn them out on to a wire rack. Serve warm with butter or cream cheese to accompany hot soups, salads or a selection of fruit and cheese.

Makes 12

Corn–Ham Muffins. Add 300 g/11 oz/1¼ cups drained corn kernels, a pinch of cayenne pepper and 60 g/2 oz/⅓ cup finely chopped ham to the dry ingredients.

Cinnamon–Apricot Muffins. Substitute the same quantity of wholemeal (wholewheat) for the plain (all-purpose) flour, adding 2 teaspoons ground cinnamon, 3 tablespoons raw sugar and 60 g/ 2 oz/½ cup dried chopped apricots.

Chocolate or Nut Muffins. Add 60 g/2 oz/¼ cup caster (superfine) sugar and 60 g/2 oz/½ cup chopped walnuts or chocolate to the dry ingredients.

Cinnamon Sugar Banana Toasts

4 slices sourdough bread, 12 x 8 x 2.5 cm/5 x 3 x	*2 eggs*
1 inch	*125 ml/4 fl oz/½ cup milk*
2 bananas	*1 teaspoon vanilla essence (extract)*
125 g/4 oz/½ cup sugar	*Vegetable oil for frying*
1 teaspoon ground cinnamon	*Plain yoghurt, to serve*

Place a flat hand on top of each bread slice, insert a small sharp knife into one side of each slice and cut out an arc shape carefully to make a pocket, leaving a 2.5 cm/1 inch border around the edge. Peel and cut the bananas crosswise and then lengthwise. Place two pieces into each pocket.

Mix together the sugar and cinnamon and leave to stand. Whisk together the eggs, milk and vanilla essence in a shallow dish. Add the bread slices and leave to soak on each side for 5 minutes or until the egg mixture is absorbed.

Heat about 5 cm/2 inches of oil in a large frying pan (skillet) until a small cube of bread turns golden. Add 2 bread slices and cook on each side for 1–2 minutes. Lift out on to a wire rack lined with paper towels. Repeat the procedure with the remaining bread slices. Sprinkle the sugar and cinnamon mixture generously over each slice and serve with plain yoghurt.
Makes 4

Baked Ham Roulades

12 fresh thick square (toasting) slices wholemeal
   (wholewheat) bread
12 squares ready-cooked ham
60 g/2 oz/½ cup mushrooms, chopped
125 g/4 oz/1 cup grated Cheddar cheese

1 egg
¼ teaspoon salt
¼ teaspoon cayenne pepper
125 g/4 oz/½ cup butter, melted
150g/5 oz/1 cup sesame seeds

Cut away the crusts from the bread and roll each slice firmly with a rolling pin. Place a square of ham on each. Mix together the mushrooms, cheese, egg, salt and pepper. Spoon the mixture on to the centre section of each square of ham and roll up. Secure with cocktail sticks (toothpicks), brush melted butter over each and sprinkle with sesame seeds. Place on a baking sheet and bake in a preheated oven at 200°C/400°F/gas 6 for 10 minutes. Turn over and bake for a further 5 minutes. Remove from the oven and take out the cocktail sticks.
Makes 12

Baked Ham Roulades

| *Cut crusts from bread slices and roll each slice firmly with a rolling pin.* | *Place a ham slice and some mushroom mixture on each slice of bread.* | *Roll up and fix with a toothpick.* | *Brush melted butter on each one and sprinkle with sesame seeds.* |

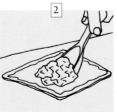

Dips and Spreads

Dips and spreads are also snacks. They can be indulgent party entertainers, simple appetizers or quick healthy meals in themselves. Served with crunchy crudités—which are simply raw vegetables—they are certainly a more refreshing eating experience than crisps and lots of nuts. You will find a list of suggested raw vegetables, some which are best lightly blanched, (see p. 26) and information on preparation. It is not necessary to buy all the vegetables specially unless you are entertaining and want to impress your friends. Crudités can be what you already have in the refrigerator but as a guide, serve 3–4 vegetable pieces per person for informal occasions and perhaps 7–9 for a party presentation.

Cheese fondue is a special kind of dip, the difference being that it is a hot, bubbling sauce traditionally served with crusty bread—however, there is no reason why you cannot include blanched vegetables as dippers too.

Cheese Fondue (p. 28) preparation. Simmering white wine assists in melting the combination of grated cheeses; cornflour prevents separation and thickens the fondue.

Crudités

Arrange a selection of the following in groups on a white china platter, or a flat basket lined with lettuce or salad leaves.

Raw Vegetables. Carrots; yellow, red or green peppers (capsicums, bell peppers); cucumber; celery cut into sticks; small button mushrooms; trimmed radishes; chicory (whitloof) leaves; cherry tomatoes.

Blanched Vegetables (p. 26). Broccoli or cauliflower florets; French (green beans), trimmed; courgettes (baby marrows, zucchini), cut into diagonal slices; small new potatoes; asparagus spears

Breads. Crusty French-style breads; small savoury muffins; sliced rye or wholemeal (whole-wheat) bread.

Aïoli

A garlic mayonnaise and sauce from the Provence region of France complements crudités, cold meats and hard-boiled eggs.

4 large garlic cloves, crushed	200–250 ml/7–8 fl oz/³⁄₄–1 cup olive oil
¼ teaspoon salt	Juice of 1 lemon
2 egg yolks	

Place the garlic, salt and egg yolks in a food processor. With the motor running, add the oil gradually in a continuous trickle until the sauce emulsifies or thickens. Blend in the lemon juice.

If you find that the aïoli begins to separate, it can be reconstituted by working it back into a fresh egg yolk. Place the yolk in a clean bowl and whisk in a little vinegar and oil until it starts to thicken. Pour in the separated mixture and continue to whisk until well combined.

Makes about 1¼ cups

How to use Stale Bread. *Arrange 8 slices in a greased heatproof dish to cover the bottom and sides. Scatter about 125 g/4 oz/1 cup of grated cheese over the bread and top with fresh herbs (include sun-dried tomatoes and olives, if liked). Beat together 4 eggs and 300 ml/½ pint/1¼ cups milk, season with salt and pepper and pour over the bread mixture. Cover and refrigerate for about 1 hour, then bake in a preheated oven at 180°C/350°F/gas 4 for 40–45 minutes and serve.*

Left: Crudités with Aïoli. A garlic mayonnaise is a classic sauce for crudités. Make it in the food processor so it is ready in no time to impress your friends.

Overleaf: Golden Herb Omelette (p. 32) (right) and Smoked Trout Egg Scramble (p.33) (left) make easy snack meals with fruit juices and coffee.

For Crudités (p. 23), always select vegetables that contrast in texture and shape. Cut into portions that can pick up the dip and are easily eaten.

Blanching Vegetables

Cut vegetables into desired shapes.	*Plunge vegetables into boiling water for 20 seconds.*	*Plunge immediately into iced water to stop further cooking.*	*Drain and use as required.*

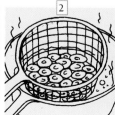
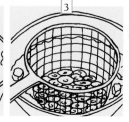
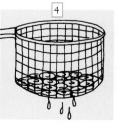

Cucumber Yoghurt

This dip is of Greek origin. Serve with crudité or crusted bread.

500 g/18 oz cucumber
3 spring onions (scallions), trimmed and
   finely sliced
3 tablespoons snipped chives
1/2 teaspoon salt

1 teaspoon sugar
Pepper
A few drops of Tabasco
250 g/8 fl oz/1 cup plain yoghurt

Cut the cucumber in half lengthwise, scoop out the pips (seeds) with a teaspoon and slice finely. Combine with the remaining ingredients and chill.

Makes about 2 cups

Chives: *Snip chives with kitchen scissors after washing thoroughly. Keep the bunch tied together to make them easier to handle.*

Middle Eastern Chick-pea Dip

Chick-pea (garbanzo bean) and sesame seed purée or dip is of Middle Eastern origin and appreciated widely. There is no need to cook dried peas as they are available canned, and ready-made tahini can be purchased in delicatessens and supermarkets.

450 g/1 lb canned chick-peas (garbanzo beans),
   drained, liquid reserved
2–3 garlic cloves, crushed
125 ml/4 fl oz/½ cup tahini
Juice of 2 lemons
Salt

3 teaspoons olive oil
1 teaspoon paprika, to garnish
1 tablespoon finely chopped parsley, to garnish
Flat pitta (Lebanese) bread, to serve
Celery sticks, to serve

Set aside 3 tablespoons of the chick-peas. Place the remainder in a food processor and blend to a smooth purée, adding some reserved liquid if the mixture becomes too dry. Spoon into a bowl. Add the garlic, tahini and lemon juice gradually, beating the mixture vigorously. Season with salt and add more lemon juice and garlic if liked.

Spoon the hummus on to a flat plate and make a shallow depression in the centre. Pour the olive oil into the centre and sprinkle with paprika. Sprinkle over parsley and reserved whole chick-peas. Serve with pitta bread and celery sticks.

Makes about 2–2½ cups

Cheese Fondue

Fondue means 'melted' in French and is also the name given to a cheese dish, melted in wine, from Switzerland. This is a sociable snack, so get your friends or family to take turns stirring the pot when the cheese is melting in the simmering wine. You can substitute other mature, firm cheeses like Cheddar, Edam and Gouda, if liked.

375 g/13 oz/3¼ cups Emmenthal cheese, coarsely
    grated
375 g/13 oz/3¼ cups Gruyère cheese, coarsely
    grated
1 tablespoon plain (all-purpose) flour
1 garlic clove, cut in half

375 ml/13 fl oz/1⅔ cups dry white wine
¼ teaspoon grated nutmeg
¼ teaspoon pepper
1 tablespoon Kirsch, if liked
Crusty bread cubes, to serve

Place the cheeses and flour in a polythene bag and toss together. Rub the inside of a flameproof casserole, ceramic fondue pot or heavy-based saucepan with the garlic halves. Discard the garlic and pour in the wine. Bring to the boil over a low heat. Stir in the cheese mixture one handful at a time, stirring continuously until each addition dissolves. Stir until the fondue is bubbling and smooth. Season with nutmeg and pepper. Add Kirsch if liked. Keep hot over a burner. Spear the bread cubes with a fork and dip into the simmering fondue.
Serves 4–6

Cheese Fondue

| Rub the inside of the fondue pot with garlic. | Pour in wine and start stirring in cheese mixture. | Stir until fondue is smooth and bubbling. Keep hot over burner. | Spear the bread cubes and dip into fondue. |

 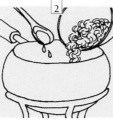  

Cheese Fondue is a wonderful snack meal when friends call in. You can dip in blanched vegetables as well as crusty bread.

Walnut Camembert

Shaped back into a round, this savoury cheese spread can also be served with hot toasted breads or bagels topped with smoked salmon.

125 g/4 oz packaged Camembert cheese
125 g/4 oz cream cheese
125 g/4 oz/1 cup shelled walnuts
30 g/1 oz/2 tablespoons butter

¼ teaspoon paprika, to garnish
Slices of rye or pumpernickel bread, to serve
Pear quarters, to serve

Allow the cheeses to come to room temperature if taken from the refrigerator. Chop both into small pieces and mash them together in a bowl with a fork or spoon until combined. Chop half the walnuts finely and stir them into the cheese mixture. Shape the mixture into a round like a hamburger, place on a platter and chill until required.

Melt the butter in a small pan, add the remaining walnuts and cook, stirring continuously, until golden. Drain on paper towels. Press the walnuts around the sides and top of the cheese round. Sprinkle lightly with paprika. Serve with bread and pears.

Serves 4

Tomato Tuna with Crostini

Juicy, red, ripe tomatoes are the essential ingredient for this delicious spread served on crisp oven-baked bread.

8 ripe tomatoes
1 teaspoon salt
1 garlic clove, crushed
1 tablespoon chopped basil
2 tablespoons Italian (flat-leaf) parsley

2 tablespoons virgin olive oil
200 g/7 oz canned tuna in oil
Pepper
12 slices country-style round Italian bread, cut
   in half, or 24 slices French bread

Place the tomatoes in a food processor and pulse at 1 second intervals until finely chopped—do not purée. Transfer the tomatoes to a sieve (strainer), mix with the salt and leave to drain. Press down using a spoon to release excess tomato juices. Place the tomato pulp in a bowl and combine with the garlic, basil and parsley. Whisk in the olive oil gradually until well blended. Fold in the tuna and season with pepper and more salt if liked. Leave to stand.

Arrange the bread slices on a flat baking sheet. Place in a preheated oven at 200°C/400°F/gas 6 and bake for about 10 minutes until crisp and golden. Place the tomato mixture in a small bowl in the centre of a platter and surround with the crostini.

Serves 4–6

Egg Snacks

R ich in protein, vitamins and minerals, eggs are well known for their nutritional benefits. They are a self-contained, universal, complete snack food served for breakfast or any light meal. It is best to purchase your eggs from a busy supermarket or store with a fast turnover so that they are as fresh as possible. Store them in the refrigerator away from highly flavoured foods as the shells are porous and absorb flavours. Always place the pointed ends down to allow the airspace at the rounded end to breathe. Where possible, it is best to have your eggs at room temperature before using, because they will beat together more easily to give good volume, and not crack when being boiled.

Tomato and basil variation to Golden Herb Omelette (p.32). Add the filling when the eggs are just setting, before folding over and turning onto the plate.

Golden Herb Omelette

This folded French-style omelette should take no longer than 1½ minutes once the egg hits the prepared pan. You will find endless fillings or sauces to add once you have mastered this technique.

3 eggs
Salt and pepper
1 tablespoon water

1 tablespoon chopped parsley or snipped chives
30 g/1 oz/2 tablespoons butter

Break the eggs into a bowl and season with salt and pepper. Add the water and half the parsley or chives, and beat with a fork just enough to mix the yolks and whites together.

Heat an 18–20 cm/7–8 inch omelette or frying pan (skillet) until hot enough to make butter sizzle on contact. Add half the butter to the heated pan and shake gently so that the butter coats the pan evenly.

When the butter sizzles but is not turning brown, pour in the egg mixture all at once. Stir for a second or two quickly to ensure even cooking. As the egg starts to set, lift the edges with a fork so the liquid can run underneath. Repeat until all the liquid is used up but the eggs are still moist and soft.

Tilt the pan away from you and loosen around the edges if necessary. Allow the omelette to slip up the far edge of the pan, then fold top half over away from the handle. Slide the omelette on to a warm plate by tilting the pan and raising the handle to release the omelette just as it touches the plate. Melt the remaining butter, toss in the remaining parsley or chives and pour over the omelette. Serve immediately.

Serves 1

Variations. Just as the egg begins to set, add one of the following: 1 tablespoon each grated Parmesan cheese and single (light) cream, or finely chopped, seeded tomato and fresh basil, or 2 tablespoons grated Cheddar or Swiss cheese.

Making an Omelette

Mix the eggs, seasonings, water and herbs thoroughly in a bowl.	Melt butter in a pan and heat until golden.	Pour in egg mixture.	Lift the edges with a fork so the liquid can run underneath and set uniformly. Fold over and serve.

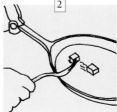

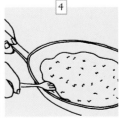

Smoked Trout Egg Scramble

A light, creamy egg snack that is perfect for breakfast or brunch with piping hot coffee or fruit juice.

250 g/9 oz smoked trout
5 eggs
4 tablespoons single (light) cream
Salt and pepper

4 thick slices light rye or sourdough bread
2 tablespoons snipped chives, to garnish
4 lime or small lemon wedges, to garnish

Cut along the backbone of the trout carefully, peel away the skin and remove the head. Remove the flesh from the backbone, using the tip of a small knife. Flake the flesh and leave to stand.

Beat together the eggs and cream and season lightly with salt and pepper. Heat a non-stick frying pan (skillet)—or, alternatively, melt 1 teaspoon of butter in a saucepan—and pour in the egg mixture. Cook over a low heat, stirring continuously, until the eggs are set but still creamy and soft. Stir in the trout.

Toast the bread on both sides and spoon over the scrambled egg mixture. Sprinkle with chives and add a wedge of the lime or lemon.
Serves 4

Piperade

Otherwise known as a tomato and pepper stew, this dish is cooked in a frying pan (skillet) with beaten eggs stirred through. Ham is added in this version.

4 ripe tomatoes
2 tablespoons olive oil
1 green pepper (capsicum, bell pepper), sliced
1 onion, sliced

1 garlic clove, crushed
60 g/2 oz/⅓ cup ham, chopped
4 eggs
Salt and pepper

Peel the tomatoes, remove the seeds and chop finely (p. 33). Heat the oil in a frying pan (skillet) and fry the pepper and onion for 2–3 minutes. Add the tomatoes, garlic and ham. Simmer, uncovered, for 20–25 minutes until the vegetables form a soft purée.

Beat the eggs and season with salt and pepper. Stir gently through the hot vegetable mixture using a fork or wooden spoon until cooked like scrambled eggs in consistency. Serve with triangles of toast or thick slices of crusty bread.
Serves 2

Peeling Tomatoes. *Use ripe tomatoes only. Cut out the core using a small knife. Plunge into boiling water for 1–2 minutes. The skin will start to lift. Refresh under cold water, peel off the skin and use as needed.*

Caesar Salad. This popular classic salad is a complete meal which may be prepared ahead of time and assembled when required. A chilled white wine makes a perfect accompaniment.

Shaving Cheese. *As an alternative to grating, shave cheese by drawing a vegetable peeler firmly over a block or piece of hard cheese such as Parmesan.*

Caesar Salad

1 large cos (romaine) lettuce
3 thin rashers (slices) bacon, rinds removed, cut
   into 2.5 cm/1 inch pieces
4 thick slices day-old white bread
60 g/2 oz/¼ cup butter
5 tablespoons olive oil
1 garlic clove, crushed
4 eggs

200 g/7 oz block Parmesan cheese
1 red pepper (capsicum, bell pepper), cut into
   fine strips
45 g/1½ oz canned anchovy fillets, drained
   and chopped
2 tablespoons lemon juice
Salt and pepper

Wash and dry the lettuce leaves and place them in a bowl. Cook the bacon in a frying pan (skillet) until crisp. Remove and drain on paper towels.

Remove and discard the bread crusts, and cut the bread into 12 mm/1/2 inch cubes. Melt the butter in a large frying pan (skillet), add 2 tablespoons of the oil and cook the garlic until it sizzles, then add the bread cubes. Shake the pan to coat the cubes and fry for about 5 minutes until golden brown. Remove the croutons and drain on paper towels.

Place the eggs in a saucepan of cold water, bring slowly to the boil, remove from the heat, cover and leave to stand for 5 minutes. Peel the softly boiled or 'coddled' eggs carefully and cut in half.

Shave the Parmesan cheese (p. 34) and add it to the lettuce in the bowl along with the bacon, pepper and anchovies, remaining oil and lemon juice. Toss together carefully and season with salt and pepper. Arrange the salad on four plates, add an egg and sprinkle over extra pepper.
Serves 4

Toss a Caesar Salad together just before you need it, adding the egg last.

Step by Step

Pizzas

There is nothing as delicious as a steaming hot pizza fragrant with oregano, garlic, rich tomato, topped with melting mozzarella cheese. The origins of pizza—which means 'pie'—can be found far back in Roman history when, as simple breads, they were baked on hot stones, clay discs and later, metal bakestones specially prepared for the purpose. Today there is a huge variety of pizzas using bases from foccacia bread to prepared frozen dough rounds. You do not have to make a yeast dough because the following recipes use simple one-bowl scone or quickbread-style mixtures. You will also find innovative toppings that are different to traditional Italian ones. As a bonus these toppings—and any that you may devise—can easily be used on thick-sliced toasted crusty breads. Always preheat the oven to the suggested temperature; a successful pizza relies on a high heat to bake the base to golden crispness.

Making a Pizza Base

Sift the flour into a bowl.	*Mix in the egg and milk to make a firm dough.*	*Place on a floured surface and knead until smooth.*	*Roll out into a circle with a rolling pin.*
	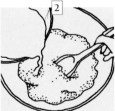		

Pissaladière

This is an easy and quick version of an onion and anchovy pizza traditionally made in Provence with a yeast dough.

4 tablespoons olive oil
5 onions, cut in half and thinly sliced
2 garlic cloves, chopped
1 teaspoon chopped thyme
1 tablespoon chopped rosemary
Salt and pepper

225 g/8 oz/2 cups self-raising (self-rising) flour
1 egg
125 ml/4 fl oz/½ cup milk
60 g/2 oz anchovy fillets in oil, drained
1–2 teaspoons tomato paste
18 black olives, stoned (pitted) and cut in half

36

Supreme Pizza Mozzarella (p. 38). A quick non-yeast dough is the base that saves time. Roast aubergine (eggplant) and tomato paste make an unusual base for the topping.

Heat 3 tablespoons of the oil in a frying pan (skillet) and add the onions, garlic and herbs. Cover and cook over a moderately low heat for 10–15 minutes, stirring regularly, until the onions are soft and a light golden colour. Season with salt and pepper. Leave to cool.

Sift the flour into a bowl and mix in the egg and milk to make a firm dough. Place the dough on a floured surface and knead until smooth. Roll out into an oblong shape measuring 30 x 25 cm/ 12 x 9 inches. Place on an oiled baking sheet.

Soak the anchovies in water for 5 minutes, drain on paper towels, then cut in half lengthwise. Cover the dough with the tomato paste to within 2.5 cm/1 inch of the rim, and spread the onion mixture over the paste. Arrange the anchovies in a lattice pattern on top and place olive halves in each section. Drizzle over the remaining oil. Place in a preheated oven at 200°C/400°F/gas 6 and bake for 12–15 minutes or until the crust is golden brown.

Serves 6

Supreme Pizza Mozzarella

This is the ultimate pizza–stretchy strands of melting mozzarella make it fun to eat.

1 large red pepper (capsicum, bell pepper)
1 aubergine (eggplant), cut in half
125 ml/4 fl oz/½ cup water
225 g/8 oz/2 cups self-raising (self-rising) flour
1 garlic clove, crushed
1 teaspoon dried basil or oregano
200 ml/7 fl oz/¾ cup milk

1 tablespoon olive oil
2 tablespoons tomato paste
125 g/4 oz salami, cut into strips
1 large tomato, sliced or cut into wedges
400 g/14 oz canned artichoke hearts, drained, cut
   into quarters
375 g/13 oz/3¼ cups mozzarella cheese, grated

Place the pepper in a shallow dish with the aubergine and water. Cover, place in a preheated oven at 200°C/400°F/gas 6 and bake for 20 minutes or until soft (do not turn the oven off). Remove covering and set aside to cool. Sift the flour into a bowl and add the garlic, herb, milk and oil. Mix to a soft dough. Place the dough on a floured surface and knead until smooth. Roll out into a circle large enough to cover an oiled 28 cm/11 inch pizza tin (pan)

Remove the seeds and skin from the pepper and cut into thick slices. Scoop out the aubergine pulp using a spoon, and place in a bowl. Combine with the tomato paste and spread over the pizza base. Arrange the remaining ingredients on top, finishing with the cheese. Place the pizza in the oven and bake for 20–25 minutes or until the crust is golden brown and the cheese has melted.
Serves 6
Variation. Substitute 200 g/7 oz drained canned sardines or tuna for the salami.

Ricotta Parmesan Pizza

Shortcrust pastry (basic pie dough) rolled out to
   line a 28 cm/11 inch pizza tin (pan)
4 tablespoons tomato paste
500 g/18 oz ricotta cheese
1 onion, thinly sliced

2 red peppers (capsicums, bell peppers),
   thinly sliced
400 g/14 oz canned prawns (shrimps), drained
125 g/4 oz/1 cup grated Parmesan cheese
Pepper

Prick pizza base well with a fork. Place in a preheated oven at 230°C/450°F/gas 8 for ten minutes to ensure a crisp base. Remove from over.

Spread tomato paste over the pizza base, arrange the ricotta cheese, onion, peppers and prawns in order, then top with the parmesan cheese. Season with the pepper.

Place in the preheated oven and bake for 10–15 minutes or until the cheese has melted.
Serves 6

Supreme Pizza Mozzarella. A very hot oven bakes this delicious Italian-style pizza in minutes.

Sun-Dried Tomato and Vegetable Pizza—choose any seasonal vegetables, brush with oil and grill (broil) until golden and tender.

Preparing Button Mushrooms. *Just wipe them with a damp cloth and trim the bases.*

Sun-Dried Tomato and Vegetable Pizza

An unusual pizza where grilled (broiled) vegetables and sun-dried tomatoes add the flavour.

1 ready-made pizza base or prepared dough
    (p. 36), about 25 cm/10 inches in diameter
5 large button mushrooms, sliced
1 onion, cut into thin wedges
1 large courgette (baby marrow, zucchini),
    cut into thin diagonal slices

3 yellow squash, thinly sliced
2 tablespoons olive oil
4–5 tablespoons tomato paste
4–6 sun-dried tomatoes, cut into strips
Lemon juice
Pepper

Place the pizza base on an oiled baking sheet. Place in a preheated oven at 230°C/450°F/gas 8 and bake for 10 minutes to ensure a crisp base (do not turn the oven off).

Brush the mushrooms, onion, courgette and squash with olive oil and grill (broil), turning frequently, until just tender but not brown.

Brush the pizza base with extra oil, spread with the tomato paste to within 2.5 cm/1 inch of the rim and arrange the vegetables on top. Return to the oven and bake for a further 8–10 minutes. Remove from the oven, scatter over the tomato strips. Squeeze over some lemon juice and season with pepper

Serves 4–6

Pesto Pizza with Smoked Salmon

Individual pizzas are fun to prepare. You can change the topping and use tomato paste with mushrooms or artichoke hearts and chèvre (goat's cheese) or feta cheese, or chopped leftover chicken and spring onions (scallions).

Shortcrust pastry (basic pie dough) rounds,
    7.5 cm/3 inches in diameter
2 tablespoons olive oil
6 tablespoons basil pesto

250 g/9 oz round Camembert or Brie
    cheese, cut into 8 wedges
250 g/9 oz smoked salmon, cut into small pieces
Basil leaves, torn, to garnish

Place the pastry rounds on oiled baking sheets. Prick the bases well with a fork and brush with the oil. Place in a preheated oven at 230°C/450°F/gas 8 and bake for 10–15 minutes to ensure a crisp base (do not turn the oven off).

Spread some of the basil pesto over each pastry round to within a 12 mm/½ inch of the rim. Top each with a Camembert wedge. Return to the oven and bake for a further 5 minutes until the cheese melts. Remove from the oven and arrange the smoked salmon and basil leaves on top.

Makes 8

Basil Pesto. Place 20 large basil leaves in a food processor and add 2 tablespoons pine nuts or almonds, 3 peeled garlic cloves, and 200 ml/7 fl oz/¾ cup olive oil. Process to a thick paste. Place in an airtight container and store in the refrigerator.

Makes about ¾ cup

Light Meal Snacks

Rice, pasta and beans are the starting point for many light meals. They are all basic larder (pantry) or store cupboard ingredients you should have on hand. In 20 minutes or so you can prepare a steaming bowl of spaghetti or fettuccine tossed with oil, garlic and grated Parmesan or cream cheese, walnuts and parsley. Canned beans are an excellent convenience food, adding nourishment to thick vegetable soups or spicy Mexican Bean Tacos. Rice, whether simply boiled or steamed, combines with a thousand and one ingredients, such as Paella. You may already have enjoyed the following recipes in a café or bistro—here is your opportunity to cook them.

Spanish Seafood Rice

Paella is the name of the round, shallow, metal container traditionally used to cook this dish. Select a wide-based, shallow cooking pan so the rice will simmer undisturbed. This version uses chicken and chorizo sausage.

30 g/1 oz/2 tablespoons butter
2 tablespoons olive oil
1 onion, finely chopped
350 g/12 oz/2 cups short-grain rice
½ teaspoon powdered saffron or turmeric, if liked
750 ml/1¼ pints/3 cups hot chicken stock

1 red pepper (capsicum, bell pepper), cut into strips
250 g/9 oz frozen peas
125 g/4 oz chorizo or pork sausage, thickly sliced
500 g/18 oz/3 cups cooked chicken, chopped
Salt and cayenne pepper
Chopped parsley, to garnish

Melt the butter in a deep, heavy-based saucepan or large frying pan (skillet). Add the oil and onion. Fry, stirring continuously, until the onion softens. Add the rice and stir continuously until the rice is coated in the butter–oil mixture.

Mix the saffron into one third of the chicken stock and add to the rice with the red peppers. Pour in the remaining chicken stock and cook, uncovered, for 15 minutes, stirring occasionally. Add the peas, chorizo and chicken, and continue cooking until the stock is absorbed and the rice is tender but still moist. Season with salt and a little cayenne pepper. Sprinkle over parsley.
Serves 4–6

Stock. *To save time prepare stock by dissolving 1 cube or teaspoon of stock powder in 250 ml/8 fl oz/1 cup hot water; mix well. Adjust proportions according to individual taste.*

Spanish Seafood Rice is a simple variation to the classic dish paella, and makes a delicious light meal.

Preparation of Spanish Seafood Rice (p. 42). Always stir the rice in the butter–oil mixture so it is well coated and golden before adding the hot stock.

Mexican Bean Tacos

A do-it-yourself snack, the filling can be prepared ahead and reheated quickly when needed. If taco shells are not available, serve on toasted rye or warm flat pitta (Lebanese) bread.

1 tablespoon oil
1 small onion, finely chopped
1 celery stick, finely chopped
1 carrot, grated
1 garlic clove, crushed
⅛–½ teaspoon chilli powder
1/2 teaspoon ground cumin
Salt and pepper

300 g/11 oz canned kidney beans
8 taco shells
2 ripe tomatoes, chopped
½ lettuce, shredded
125 g/4 oz/1 cup coarsely grated Cheddar cheese
1 avocado, cut into cubes, to serve
3 tablespoons soured cream, to serve

Heat the oil in a frying pan (skillet) and fry the onion, celery, carrot and garlic for 2–3 minutes, stirring continuously. Add the spices and season with salt and pepper. Cook for a further 2 minutes, adding a little water if the mixture becomes too dry. Stir in the beans, mashing them slightly until the mixture combines. Adjust the seasonings if necessary.

Spoon about 3 tablespoons of bean filling into each taco shell and top with some tomato, lettuce and cheese. Serve avocado and soured cream separately.

Serves 4

Basic Pasta

Pasta must be cooked in a lot of water so it moves freely. The water should be boiling and salted before adding the pasta. It should always be served hot and *al dente*, which means soft on the outside but still slightly firm to the bite.

To cook 250 g/9 oz pasta, fill a large saucepan with 2 litres/3½ pints/2¼ quarts water. Bring the water to a rolling boil, add a splash of oil and a good pinch of salt, and add the pasta. Give it a stir. Cover the pot and as soon as the water returns to a boil, stir the pasta again. Cover partially and continue cooking until the pasta is *al dente*. This will take about 10 minutes for dried pasta and 2–3 minutes for fresh pasta. Drain well in a colander. Rinse in cold water if not being used immediately.

To test if pasta is cooked: pull a piece from the water and taste it—it should be firm to the bite with no hard, white central core.

Serves 3–4

Leftover pasta. Pasta can be reheated in a pan with some butter, removed and seasoned with salt, pepper and chopped herbs or grated cheese.

Seeding Tomatoes (Concasse). *Peel the tomatoes (p. 33) and cut them in half. Squeeze the tomato gently, or scoop out the pips (seeds) with a teaspoon. Flatten each half gently and cut into small cubes. Use as required.*

Basil Mint Minestra

A very easy, hearty soup accented with fresh basil and mint leaves.

1 tablespoon olive oil	Salt and pepper
1 onion, chopped	400 g/14 oz canned borlotti or cannellini beans,
125 g/4 oz Parma ham (prosciutto) or lean bacon,	drained
chopped	20 basil leaves, torn
1.5 litres/2¾ pints/7 cups chicken stock	20 mint or Italian (flat-leaf) parsley leaves, torn
250 g/9 oz spaghetti, broken into 5 cm/2 inch	
lengths	

Heat the oil in a large saucepan. Add the onions and ham and fry over a low heat for 5 minutes. Add the stock and bring to the boil. Add the spaghetti, season with salt, stir and boil for about 10 minutes or until *al dente* (p. 47). Add the beans and season with pepper. Add the basil and mint and serve immediately.

Serves 4

Tuna Fish and Black Olive Pasta

An appetizing, simple dish using ingredients from your larder (pantry) that can be prepared in 20 minutes or less. A bowl brimming with tossed lettuce leaves and vegetables of your choice will complete this pasta meal.

4 tablespoons olive oil
1 onion, chopped
2 garlic cloves, chopped
12 black olives, stoned (pitted) (p. 14)
400 g/14 oz canned whole peeled tomatoes,
  drained and chopped

¼ teaspoon dried oregano
200 g/7 oz canned tuna, drained
Salt and pepper
400 g/14 oz penne, shell or rigatoni pasta

Heat the oil in a saucepan and add the onion, garlic and olives. Cook, stirring regularly, for 5 minutes until the onion softens. Stir in the tomatoes and simmer for 15 minutes. Add the oregano and tuna, stir lightly and season with salt and pepper. Leave to simmer for a further 2–3 minutes.

Meanwhile, cook the pasta in boiling salted water until *al dente* (p. 47), then transfer to a warm bowl. Pour over the sauce, mix together and serve immediately.

Serves 4

Heating Oil. *Oil is hot when it starts to ripple in a pan and a piece of food dropped into it sizzles, with bubbles forming around it. Very hot oil will start to smoke.*

Cooking Pasta

| *Put pasta into fast boiling salted water.* | *Stir and add a splash of oil.* | *Partially cover the pot and cook pasta until* al dente. | *Drain well in a colander and serve.* |

Spaghetti Carbonara

One of the simplest snacks to make, carbonara means eggs and bacon tossed through hot pasta. The addition of cream with the beaten eggs and cheese is an option, but it does give this dish an extra touch of creaminess.

400 g/14 oz spaghetti
4 eggs, beaten
125 g/4 oz/1 cup grated Parmesan cheese
Pinch of grated nutmeg
4 tablespoons single (light) cream, if liked

Salt and pepper
60 g/2 oz/¼ cup butter
200 g/7 oz rashers (slices) bacon, rinds removed,
*   chopped*
Chopped parsley, to garnish

Cook the spaghetti in boiling salted water until *al dente* (p. 47). Meanwhile, whisk together the eggs and cheese and add the nutmeg, cream, salt and plenty of pepper. Melt the butter in a frying pan (skillet) and fry the bacon quickly until slightly crisp.

Drain the spaghetti and pour into a warm bowl. Add the egg mixture and mix together quickly, using 2 spoons, so that the eggs are just cooked. Add the bacon, mix again and sprinkle over the parsley. Serve immediately.

Serves 4

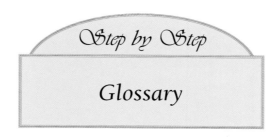

Step by Step

Glossary

Al dente Literally the Italian for 'to the tooth'. The phrase is used to describe the texture of food, usually applied to pasta, when properly cooked and just firm to the bite.

Baking powder Raising agent used in baking.

Bocconcini Mild, white, soft cheese shaped into small individual balls.

Borlotti beans Also known as Roman or red beans in England, they are round in shape and speckled.

Bruschetta Toasted bread rubbed with a cut garlic clove, then drenched in olive oil and sprinkled with salt crystals.

Camembert White, mould-surface ripened cheese with a creamy interior.

Cannellini beans Pale cream-coloured, kidney-shaped beans which have a delicate flavour.

Capers Pickled buds of a Mediterranean shrub.

Chick-peas Known also as garbanzo beans. They should be drained, washed in running water, then drained again.

Chorizo Spanish and Mexican spicy pork sausage seasoned with garlic, chilli and cayenne pepper. If unavailable, use a spicy salami.

Coarse-grain French mustard French-style mustard with crushed seeds.

Crostini Cubes or round slices of fried bread.

Emmenthal cheese Quick- melting, sweet, nutty-tasting cheese.

Floret Broccoli or cauliflower, broken or cut into small pieces with no or little stalk.

Gruyère cheese Swiss cheese with small holes and a nutty, slightly salty flavour.

Kirsch An alcohol used in the preparation of fondues and some cakes.

Mortadella Pinkish delicatessen sausage made from pork, which has large white spots and sometimes contains pistachio nuts.

Mozzarella Light yellow, smooth, mild-textured and excellent melting cheese used on pizzas and in cooking.

Parma ham (Prosciutto Uncooked, cured ham which is not smoked.

Parmesan cheese Usually eaten with pasta. It is a golden, crumbly, hard grating cheese made from cow's milk. Best purchased in a block, then grated or shaved.

Pimentos Sweet red peppers preserved in brine in cans or jars.

Pitta (Lebanese) bread Layered flat bread, prepared without a raising (rising) agent, cut to form a pocket.

Purée Press a cooked food through a sieve (strainer) or put into a blender or food processor to produce a smooth thick mixture.

Ricotta cheese Mild-flavoured fresh cheese which is soft, white and creamy, used in savoury and sweet dishes or as a spread.

Red kidney beans Beans with a floury texture and fairly sweet flavour, the colour varying from light red to maroon.

Saffron Yellow colouring obtained from the stamens of a species of crocus, available in ground or strand form.

Sauerkraut Shredded cabbage fermented with salt and flavoured with juniper berries, often accompanying preserved meats.

Sourdough bread Very dense, heavy-textured bread prepared by extensive fermentation.

Sun-dried tomatoes Tomatoes dried in the sun, having a concentrated, salty flavour, commonly bottled in oil.

Tabasco Sauce made with vinegar, hot red peppers and salt.

Tahini paste Made from sesame seeds, available from health food shops and delicatessens.

Worcestershire sauce Spicy sauce made from vinegar, anchovies, molasses and spices, commonly accompanying meat dishes.